LOVE'S UNCONDITIONAL REVOLUTION:

UNLEASH AND IGNITE THE TRANSFORMATIVE POWER OF LOVE

Love Has Everything To Do With It!
Written by Alisa L. Grace

Love's Unconditional Revolution

Unleash and Ignite the Transformative Power of Love

Written by
Alisa L. Grace

© 2025 Alisa L. Grace

All rights reserved.

No part of this book may be reproduced in any form or by any electronic or mechanical means, including information storage and retrieval systems, without permission in writing from the publisher.

Self-Published by

Alisa L. Grace

Sanford, FL 32771

ISBN: 978-1-966129-76-9

First Edition

Printed in the United States of America

Library of Congress Cataloging-in-Publication Data

Grace, Alisa L.

Title of the Book: Love's Unconditional Revolution: Unleash and Ignite the Transformative Power of Love

Library of Congress Control Number: 2025903463

Disclaimer: The views expressed in this book are those of the author and do not necessarily reflect any organizations or individuals mentioned.

Acknowledgments: The author wishes to thank God, Her Husband (Linion), Victory Temple of God, Florida SPECS, Unity Youth Association, All About Serving You, Angels-ANJ Events, NordeVest, and Love & Create Life for their support and contributions.

This book is dedicated to:

My Heavenly Father who has given me the task of writing about true love.

My Husband who has supported me on this book-writing journey.

My children and grandchildren whom I adore and love dearly.

To the readers of this book: may the transformative power of God's love change your life in every aspect.

Love Has Everything to Do With It!

-Yours Truly

Table of Contents

Why Should I Read Another Book About Love? 11

Introduction 15

Overview of 1 Corinthians 13:4-7 17

The Foundation of Love: 1 Corinthians 13 19

Chapter 1 Love: A Conflict between the World and the Bible 21
- Breaking Free From the Constraints of Worldly Love Expectations 24
- Transformative Questions to Ponder: 25
- Learning to Love Like Jesus: Embracing Selflessness, Forgiveness, and Compassion 27
- Transformative Questions to Ponder: 29
- The Love of Jesus: An Exemplary Model (1 Corinthians 13:4-7) 31
- Please complete the Exemplary Love Survey: Reflecting on Christ-like Love in Action. 33
- Exemplary Love Survey: Reflecting on Christ-like Love in Action 34

Chapter 2 Understanding Love's Essence 37
- Love's Portrait: Unveiling the Divine Essence of Love Through 1 Corinthians 13:4-7 41
- Transformative Questions to Ponder 43
- The Transformative Power of Kindness: Healing Relationships and Building a Better World 45
- Transformative Questions to Ponder: 47
- The Humility Imperative: Counteracting the 'Me-First' Mentality 49
- Transformative Questions To Ponder: 52
- Selflessness: Sacrificing for the well-being of others. 54
- Transformative Questions To Ponder: 57
- Forgiveness: Letting go of resentment and extending grace. 59
- Transformative Questions to Ponder: 61
- Perseverance: Remaining Steadfast In Love Despite Challenges. 63
- Transformative Supports for Your Marriage: 64
- Transformative Supports for Your Workplace: 65
- Transformative Supports for Your Community Interactions: 66
- Transformative Questions to Ponder: 67

Chapter 3 Love in Action: Practicing Unconditional Love 69

Applying Love In Various Situations and Relationships (Verses 4-7). 72

Transformative Questions to Ponder: 74

Love Unveiled: Everyday Encounters Illuminating Acts of Kindness 76

Transformative Questions to Ponder: 78

Love's Revolution: Transforming Every Aspect of Life with a Mindset of Compassion 80

Transformative Questions to Ponder: 87

Chapter 4 Overcoming Obstacles to Love 89

Identifying and Addressing Obstacles to Love (Verse 5). 92

Understanding the Role of Anger and Resentment in Hindering Love: 93

Practicing Forgiveness and Reconciliation in Relationships: 95

Transformative Questions to Ponder: 96

Chapter 5 The Ripple Effect: Spreading Love in a World of Hate 99

Transformative Questions To Ponder: 102

Creating a Ripple Effect of Positivity and Kindness: 104

Transformative Questions to Ponder: 105

Examining the Impact of Love On Communities and Societies 107

Transformative Questions to Ponder: 108

Inspiring Others to Embrace Love as a Guiding Principle of Social Change. 110

Transformative Questions to Ponder 111

Survey Your Transformative Journey 113

Live the Love You Have Learned: Love Letter To The Readers 115

Meet The Author 117

Back Book Cover Summary .... ¡Error! Marcador no definido.

Why Should I Read Another Book About Love?

Love is a compelling force that can transform lives and change the world when used as it was divinely designed: to love beyond conditions. At the core of love is 1 Corinthians 13, a chapter in the Bible that describes the practical principles of love. Here's the truth: We have all been conditioned to love conditionally from birth. How, you may ask?

Many forms of media, such as songs, books, TV shows, social media, and toxic relationships, can all contribute to conditioning us to love conditionally. These platforms can create unrealistic expectations and perpetuate the idea that love is based on external factors like attractiveness, success, or popularity. Toxic relationships often use love as a tool for manipulation or control, leading individuals to believe that love must be earned through obedience or meeting the needs of the other person. Media and social platforms can also foster a culture of comparison and competition, leading to a mindset of conditional love where affection is contingent upon outperforming others or maintaining a certain image. Additionally, the media often portrays an idealized version of love that may not reflect the complexities of genuine relationships, leading people to struggle to accept love that doesn't meet these standards. By being mindful of these influences, individuals can recognize and challenge conditional attitudes toward love, fostering healthier and more authentic relationships.

If you want to tap into the power of love and apply it to your life, read Love's Unconditional Revolution! "Unleash and Ignite the Transformative Power of Love."

This incredible book takes you on a journey to discover how the practical principles of love in 1 Corinthians 13 can be applied to every aspect of your life. From relationships to work, personal growth to spirituality, you will be amazed at how much your life can change once you apply these principles. So, are you ready to unlock the power of true love and transform your life? Let the journey begin.

Dear Reader,

As you delve into the pages of "Love's Unconditional Revolution," prepare to embark on a transformative journey that will reshape your understanding and experience of love. This book is more than just a collection of ideas; it's an invitation to a revolution that begins within your heart and ripples outward to touch the lives of those around you.

To deepen this experience and support you in implementing these principles, I've created a companion journal: **The 30-Day Challenge: Transformative Living—Love's Unconditional Revolution Journal.**

This journal is designed to guide you as you integrate the concepts of unconditional love into your daily life. Within its pages, you'll find:

- **Daily prompts:** Thought-provoking questions and reflections to inspire personal growth and action.
- **Space for journaling:** There is ample room to record your thoughts, feelings, and insights as you progress through the challenge.
- **A framework for action:** Guidance on applying the principles of unconditional love to your relationships and interactions with the world.

Whether you use this journal alongside the book or as a standalone tool, it will be a powerful catalyst for change. It will challenge you to:

- **Examine your own beliefs and behaviors around love.**
- **Identify areas where you can cultivate greater compassion, patience, and forgiveness.**
- **Take concrete steps to express unconditional love to yourself and others.**

The 30-Day Challenge is an opportunity to embody the transformative power of love truly. It's a chance to create a ripple effect of kindness, starting with your own heart and extending outward to touch the world.

I invite you to embrace this journey with an open mind and a willingness to grow. Let this book and its companion journal be your guides as you unleash the revolutionary power of unconditional love.

With anticipation for the journey ahead,

Your Sister in Love

Introduction

In a world marred by division, strife, and discord, the timeless message of love stands as a beacon of hope and transformation. Welcome to *"Love's Unconditional Revolution - Unleash and Ignite the Transformative Power of Love."* As we embark on this journey together, let us first glance at the table of contents, which serves as a roadmap for exploring love's profound significance.

Table of Contents:

- Love: A Conflict between the World and The Bible
- Understanding Love's Essence
- Love in Action: Practicing Unconditional Love
- Overcoming Obstacles to Love
- The Ripple Effect: Spreading Love in a World of Hate

In a world inundated with messages of self-interest and division, it's easy to feel disillusioned by the state of affairs. The absence of genuine love is evident, from conflicts between nations to discord within communities and even strife within families. We witness this lovelessness in the headlines, our workplaces, and sometimes even our hearts.

But what if we told you the solution to this pervasive lovelessness lies within our grasp? What if we could transform our world, one heart at a time, simply by embracing and embodying the profound truth that "Love has everything to do with it"?

In this introductory exploration, let us ponder some questions together:

- What does it mean to love others, as outlined in 1 Corinthians 13:4-7 truly?
- How can we cultivate a deeper understanding of love's essence and its transformative power?
- What obstacles stand in the way of us embodying unconditional love in our daily lives?
- How can we, as individuals, initiate a ripple effect of love that permeates every aspect of our world?

Throughout our journey, we'll draw from the timeless wisdom of 1 Corinthians 13:4-7 and other scriptures illuminating the profound nature of love. From the words of Jesus to the teachings of ancient sages, we'll uncover a rich tapestry of insights that inspire and guide us on our quest to unlock the power of love.

So, let us embark on this odyssey together, with open hearts and eager minds, as we uncover love's transformative potential and ability to heal, unite, and uplift humanity. As we shall discover, love has everything to do with it.

Overview of 1 Corinthians 13:4-7

Love's Unconditional Revolution - Unleash the Transformative Power of Love: Unlocking the Limitless Potential of 1 Corinthians 13:4-7 delves into the profound teachings of love found in the timeless scriptures. Drawing primarily from 1 Corinthians 13, this book guides you through a journey to uncover the transformative essence of love and its practical application in our lives.

The foundation of this exploration lies in the initial verses of 1 Corinthians 13, where the importance of love is emphasized over spiritual gifts and acts of service devoid of love. From this foundational understanding, the book progresses to delve into the essence of love as described in verses 4-7, which provide a detailed and illuminating description of love's qualities. These qualities, including suffering, patience, kindness, humility, selflessness, forgiveness, and perseverance, serve as a roadmap for understanding love's essence and embodying it in our daily lives.

Moving beyond theoretical understanding, this book explores how love manifests in action, illustrating through verses 4-7 how love behaves in various situations and relationships. It also addresses the obstacles to love, such as anger and holding grudges, offering insights on overcoming these barriers and cultivating a more profound, unconditional love.

Moreover, the book highlights the ripple effect of love, showing how love's characteristics can serve as a model for spreading positivity and kindness in a world often marred by hate and division. Finally, while rooted in 1 Corinthians 13, " Love's Unconditional Revolution- Unleash the Transformative Power of Love: Unlocking the Limitless Potential of 1 Corinthians 13:4-7" also draws from other scriptures about love, such as John 13:34-35, to provide additional insights into the nature and importance of love.

Through thoughtful exploration and discussion, this book offers readers a transformative journey into the heart of love, inspiring them to embrace love as both a guiding principle and a powerful force for change in their lives and the world around them.

The Foundation of Love: 1 Corinthians 13

Verses 1-3 emphasize the importance of love over spiritual gifts and acts of service without love.

    Understanding Love's Essence

Verses 4-7 provide a detailed description of love, highlighting its qualities such as patience, kindness, humility, selflessness, forgiveness, and perseverance.

    Love in Action: Practicing Unconditional Love

Verses 4-7 emphasize the practical aspects of love, illustrating how love behaves in various situations and relationships.

    Overcoming Obstacles to Love

Verse 5 mentions that love is not easily angered, which can be seen as an obstacle to love. Additionally, the concept of love keeping no record of wrongs (verse 5) speaks to overcoming past grievances that hinder love.

    The Ripple Effect: Spreading Love in a World of Hate

Verses 4-7, which describe love's characteristics, can serve as a model for spreading love and creating a ripple effect of positivity and kindness.

    Scriptures of Love: Insights from the Word

While not directly from 1 Corinthians 13, other scriptures about love, such as John 13:34-35 ("A new command I give you: Love one another. As I have loved you, so you must love one another. By this everyone will know that you are my disciples, if you love one another."), can provide additional insights into the nature and importance of love.

LOVE: A CONFLICT BETWEEN THE WORLD AND THE BIBLE

Breaking Free From the Constraints of Worldly Love Expectations:

Chapter 1
Love: A Conflict between the World and the Bible

Matthew 5:46-47 (MSG)

43-47 "You're familiar with the old written law, 'Love your friend,' and its unwritten companion, 'Hate your enemy.' I'm challenging that. I'm telling you to love your enemies. Let them bring out the best in you, not the worst. When someone gives you a hard time, respond with the supple moves of prayer, for then you are working out of your true selves, your God-created selves. This is what God does. He gives his best—the sun to warm and the rain to nourish—to everyone, regardless: the good and bad, the nice and nasty. Do you expect a bonus if all you do is love the lovable? Anybody can do that. Do you expect a medal if you simply say hello to those who greet you? Any run-of-the-mill sinner does that.

Love: A Conflict between the World and the Bible

God demonstrated the love described in 1 Corinthians 13 through his son, Jesus Christ. What human being do you know who would willingly go through what Jesus did for us, from leading up to the cross to being crucified, simply because of love? As the Bible explains, love is an action word that requires effort and display. On the other hand, the world perceives love as something that is received and makes them feel good. Therefore, there is a conflict between the Bible's and the world's views on love.

Breaking Free From the Constraints of Worldly Love Expectations

In today's society, we are often taught to love those who love us back and to offer affection and care in return for similar treatment. However, this concept of love usually comes with certain conditions that can harm our relationships with others.

What happens when love is not reciprocated, or someone does not meet our expectations? These questions are often overlooked because conditional love is so prevalent in our everyday lives. It is promoted in songs, on TV, and on social media and taught directly and indirectly by parents and other role models.

But is this really what love should be about? In Matthew 5:46-47, Jesus challenges this conditional mindset by saying, "If you love those who love you, what reward will you get? Are not even the tax collectors doing that? And if you greet only your people, what are you doing more than others? Do not even pagans do that?"

Here, Jesus confronts the notion that love should be reserved only for those who deserve it or can offer something in return. He urges his followers to embrace a higher standard of love that transcends worldly boundaries and embraces all people, regardless of their actions or affiliations.

God's love provides an example of this unconditional love. It does not depend on our worthiness or ability to reciprocate. Instead, it is a love that surpasses understanding, reaching out to the broken, the lost, and the marginalized. It is a love that knows no bounds, extending even to those who may seem unlovable in the eyes of the world.

As we navigate the complexities of love, let us look to God as the ultimate example of unconditional love. Let us strive to love as He loves, breaking free from the constraints of worldly expectations and embracing the transformative power of love that knows no limits. Doing so builds stronger, more meaningful relationships with those around us and creates a more loving and compassionate world.

Transformative Questions to Ponder:

1. How does embracing unconditional love challenge my preconceptions about who deserves love and how love should be given?

   _____
   _____
   _____
   _____
   _____
   _____
   _____

2. In what ways do I currently limit my love and affection based on others' actions or affiliations, and how might breaking free from these constraints enrich my relationships?

   _____
   _____
   _____
   _____
   _____
   _____
   _____

3. Reflecting on the example of God's unconditional love, how can I actively cultivate a love that transcends worldly boundaries and embraces all people, regardless of their perceived worthiness or ability to reciprocate?

_____
_____
_____
_____
_____
_____
_____

Learning to Love Like Jesus:
Embracing Selflessness, Forgiveness, and Compassion

The world's view of love often focuses on personal gain and satisfaction. Love is usually seen as a feeling or emotion rather than a selfless act of service. In contrast, Jesus' love was characterized by patience, kindness, humility, forgiveness, and selflessness. He prioritized the needs of others above his own, always seeking to serve and help those around him. In today's world, love is often conditional, based on what one can get in return. However, Jesus' love was unconditional, even to those who rejected and betrayed him. His example challenges us to redefine our understanding of love, to prioritize service over self-interest, and to live a life of sacrificial love and compassion towards others.

Many selfless and compassionate actions characterize the love exemplified by Jesus. It is a patient and long-suffering love, as seen in Jesus' dealings with his disciples' doubts and shortcomings and his endurance of hostility and rejection from those he came to save. His love is kind and compassionate, as he showed kindness to everyone he encountered, healing the sick, comforting the brokenhearted, and forgiving sinners. Jesus' love is not envious, as he never coveted what others had but instead taught contentment and generosity, urging his followers to focus on spiritual riches rather than earthly possessions.

His love is characterized by humility, as he never boasted or displayed pride, even though he deserved all honor and glory as the Son of God. Jesus' love is respectful and dignified, treating every individual with dignity and respect, irrespective of social status, ethnicity, or background. His love is selfless, as he constantly prioritized the needs of others above his comfort and desires, serving and exemplifying sacrificial love. He remained patient and slow to anger, even when confronting religious hypocrisy or injustice, often responding with grace and compassion. Jesus' love is forgiving, as he demonstrated forgiveness in its purest form, teaching his followers to forgive others as God has forgiven them.

He offered reconciliation and restoration to those who had sinned against him. Jesus' love is characterized by truth, as he embodied truth itself and consistently proclaimed the truth of God's kingdom. He rejoiced in seeing people come to know and embrace the truth, even when it challenged societal norms or personal beliefs. His love is unwavering and steadfast, exemplifying unparalleled love and commitment to humanity, even in the face of rejection, betrayal, and suffering.

Transformative Questions to Ponder:

1. How does Jesus' example of love challenge my current understanding of love as primarily focused on personal gain or satisfaction, and how can I shift towards a more selfless and compassionate approach to love in my own life?

   _____
   _____
   _____
   _____
   _____
   _____
   _____

2. Reflecting on Jesus' qualities of patience, kindness, humility, and forgiveness, in what areas of my life do I struggle to embody these characteristics in my relationships with others, and how can I cultivate these qualities to reflect Jesus' love better?

   _____
   _____
   _____
   _____
   _____
   _____
   _____

3. Jesus' love transcended societal boundaries and expectations, treating all individuals with dignity, respect, and compassion. How can I follow Jesus'

example in valuing and serving others regardless of their social status, ethnicity, or background, and how might this transform my interactions and relationships?

_____
_____
_____
_____
_____
_____
_____

The Love of Jesus: An Exemplary Model
(1 Corinthians 13:4-7)

Jesus, the embodiment of love, exemplified the qualities described in 1 Corinthians 13 throughout his life and ministry:

- **Patience (long-suffering)**: Jesus demonstrated patience in various situations, such as when he dealt with his disciples' doubts and shortcomings or endured hostility and rejection from those he came to save.
- **Kindness:** Jesus showed kindness to everyone he encountered, whether healing the sick, comforting the brokenhearted, or forgiving sinners. Acts of compassion and mercy marked his ministry.
- **Not envying:** Jesus never coveted what others had. Instead, he taught contentment and generosity, urging his followers to focus on spiritual riches rather than earthly possessions.
- **Not boasting, not proud:** Although Jesus deserved all honor and glory as the Son of God, he displayed humility throughout his life. He washed his disciples' feet, associated with the lowly, and he submitted humbly to the will of the Father, even unto death on the cross.
- **Not dishonoring others:** Jesus consistently treated people with dignity and respect, irrespective of their social status, ethnicity, or background. He valued every individual as being made in God's image.
- **Not self-seeking:** Jesus lived a life of selflessness, constantly prioritizing the needs of others above his comfort and desires. He came not to be served but to serve, exemplifying sacrificial love.
- **Not easily angered:** Though Jesus displayed righteous anger at times, such as when confronting religious hypocrisy or injustice, he was also remarkably patient and slow to anger, often responding with grace and compassion.

- **Keeping no record of wrongs:** Jesus demonstrated forgiveness in its purest form, teaching his followers to forgive others as God has forgiven them. He offered reconciliation and restoration to those who had sinned against him.
- **Rejoicing in the truth:** Jesus embodied truth itself and consistently proclaimed the truth of God's kingdom. He rejoiced in seeing people come to know and embrace the truth, even when it challenged societal norms or personal beliefs.
- **Always protecting, trusting, hoping, and persevering:** Jesus exemplified unwavering love and commitment to humanity, even in the face of rejection, betrayal, and suffering. He never wavered in trusting the Father's plan and remained steadfast in his mission to redeem humanity.

In summary, Jesus perfectly embodied the love described in 1 Corinthians 13, serving as the ultimate example of selfless, sacrificial, and unconditional love.

Please complete the Exemplary Love Survey: Reflecting on Christ-like Love in Action.

This survey is critical because it prompts self-reflection on the qualities of love exemplified by Jesus Christ as described in 1 Corinthians 13:4-7. By reflecting on these attributes, you can assess your attitudes and behaviors concerning love, identify areas for growth, and consider practical steps to embody a more Christ-like love in your interactions with others. The survey allows you to deepen your understanding of love as a selfless, sacrificial, and unconditional commitment to serving and uplifting others.

Directions for the Survey:

1. **Take your time**: Set aside a quiet moment to reflect on each question and contemplate your responses.

2. **Be honest**: Answer each question truthfully, acknowledging strengths and areas for improvement in your expression of love.

3. **Consider examples:** Draw from personal experiences or observations to enrich your responses and make them more meaningful.

4. **Ponder the implications**: After completing the survey, reflect on your answers and consider how to apply the insights gained to your daily interactions and relationships.

5. **Embrace growth:** Use the survey as a tool for personal growth and transformation, striving to embody the qualities of love exemplified by Jesus Christ.

Exemplary Love Survey: Reflecting on Christ-like Love in Action

1. **Patience**: Reflecting on Jesus' patience in various situations, consider a recent instance where you felt impatient or frustrated. How might approaching that situation with patience have led to a different outcome?

2. **Kindness**: Consider when someone shows you unexpected kindness or compassion. How did that act of kindness impact you, and how can you express that kindness in your interactions with others?

3. **Not envying**: In what areas of your life do you compare or covet what others have? How can you cultivate contentment and gratitude for your life's blessings?

4. **Not boasting, not proud**: Consider a recent achievement or success. How can you acknowledge and celebrate your accomplishments while remaining humble and recognizing the contributions of others?

5. **Not dishonoring others**: Reflect on when you felt respected and valued by someone else. How can you extend that same dignity and respect to those around you, regardless of their background or status?

6. **Not self-seeking**: Consider a situation where you could prioritize someone else's needs over your desires. How might choosing selflessness in that moment strengthen your relationships and demonstrate love?

7. **Not easily angered:** Recall a recent conflict or disagreement. How might approaching the situation gracefully and with compassion lead to a more constructive resolution?

8. **Keeping no record of wrongs:** Reflect on a past hurt or offense. How can you practice forgiveness and release any lingering resentment or bitterness?

9. **Rejoicing in the truth:** Consider when you had to confront a complicated truth or challenge a misconception. How can you embrace truth in your own life and encourage others to do the same?

10. **Always protecting, trusting, hoping, and persevering:** Reflect on a moment of adversity or hardship. How did you demonstrate resilience and perseverance, and how can you trust God's plan even during challenging times?

After completing the survey, take some time to ponder your responses and consider how you can apply the principles of love exemplified by Jesus in your daily life.

UNDERSTANDING LOVE'S ESSENCE

Enduring with Grace and Forbearance:

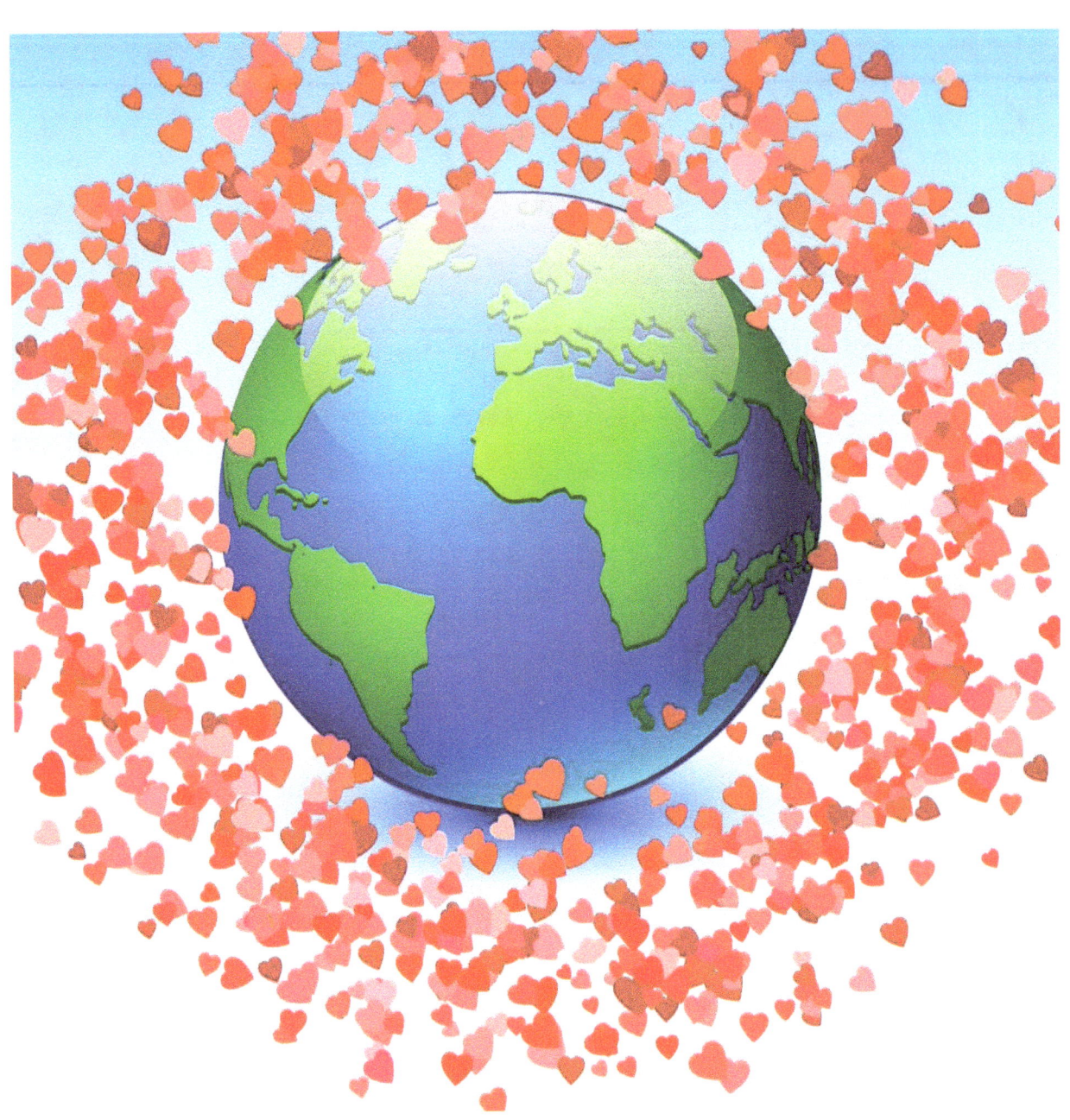

Chapter 2
Understanding Love's Essence

1 Corinthians 13:1-7 *(MSG)*

13 If I speak with human eloquence and angelic ecstasy **but don't love**, I'm nothing but the creaking of a rusty gate.

2 If I speak God's Word with power, revealing all his mysteries and making everything plain as day, and if I have faith that says to a mountain, "Jump," and it jumps, but I **don't love**, I'm nothing.

3-7 If I give everything I own to the poor and even go to the stake to be burned as a martyr, but I **don't love**, I've gotten nowhere. So, no matter what I say, what I believe, and what I do, **I'm bankrupt without love.**

Love never gives up.

Love cares more for others than for self.

Love doesn't want what it doesn't have.

Love doesn't strut,

Doesn't have a swelled head,

It doesn't force itself on others,

Isn't always "me first,"

Doesn't fly off the handle,

Doesn't keep score of the sins of others,

Doesn't revel when others grovel,

Takes pleasure in the flowering of truth,

Puts up with anything,

Trusts God always,

Always looks for the best,

Never looks back,

But keeps going to the end.

Love's Portrait:
Unveiling the Divine Essence of Love Through 1 Corinthians 13:4-7

Enduring Love: The Virtue of Patience in Building Lasting Relationships

You might wonder how patience and love are related. The answer is that they are inseparable! Patience and love are two essential virtues closely related to each other. As the Bible says in 1 Corinthians 13:4, "Love is patient, love is kind." The relationship between patience and love is inseparable since patience is fundamental to expressing love and care toward others.

Additionally, Proverbs 19:11 states, "Good sense makes one slow to anger, and it is his glory to overlook an offense." When we are patient with someone, we show them that we value their feelings and are willing to listen and understand them. Similarly, when we show love and care towards someone, we are naturally more patient with them. Therefore, patience and love go hand in hand and are essential for building strong and healthy relationships with others.

We have established that patience and love are deeply intertwined and can profoundly impact our daily relationships. As we strive to love one another with brotherly affection and show honor to those around us, we must also practice patience, seeking to understand and empathize with others even when it's difficult. As the apostle Paul wrote in Colossians 3:12-13, "Put on then, as God's chosen ones, holy and beloved, compassionate hearts, kindness, humility, meekness, and patience, bearing with one another and, if one has a complaint against another, forgiving each other; as the Lord has forgiven you, so you also must forgive." These scriptures remind us to approach others with kindness, compassion, and humility, bearing with one another's faults and forgiving one another as Christ has forgiven us.

When we approach others with patience and love, we can prevent frustration and anger from escalating and causing further harm to the relationship. We express care and concern for others through active listening, acknowledging their feelings, and seeking to understand their perspectives. Through these actions, we can build trust and strengthen our relationships with others. By letting all we do be done in love and outdoing one another in showing honor, we create a positive ripple effect in our daily interactions. We can inspire others to follow our example, cultivating a culture of patience and love in our homes, workplaces, and communities. Incorporating these virtues into our daily relationships takes practice and intentionality, but the rewards are immeasurable. As we strive to love one another with compassion, kindness, humility, meekness, and patience, we can foster stronger, healthier, and more fulfilling connections with those around us, creating a more harmonious and loving world.

Transformative Questions to Ponder:

1. Reflecting on a recent interaction where patience was tested, how did practicing patience impact the dynamics of the relationship, and what insights did you gain about the connection between patience and love?

   _____
   _____
   _____
   _____
   _____
   _____
   _____

2. Consider a challenging relationship where patience seems particularly difficult to maintain. How might embodying qualities like kindness, humility, and compassion, as outlined in Colossians 3:12-13, help to cultivate patience and foster reconciliation in that relationship?

   _____
   _____
   _____
   _____
   _____
   _____
   _____

3. Think about when you observed someone else demonstrating patience and love in their interactions. How did their example influence your perspective on the importance of patience in building lasting relationships, and what steps can you take to emulate that example in your own interactions?

_____
_____
_____
_____
_____
_____
_____

The Transformative Power of Kindness: Healing Relationships and Building a Better World

In today's world, hate, unforgiveness, resentment, and anger seem rampant. Compassion and empathy seem outdated concepts. Yet kindness is a powerful way to express love that can heal hurt, ease pain, solve issues, and create loving environments.

Kindness, compassion, and empathy are essential qualities that we need to cultivate in our daily lives. They can have a profound impact on our relationships, our work, and our world. We open ourselves to healing, growth, and connection when we show kindness, compassion, and empathy. Kindness can transform a child's experiences outside a reckless or neglectful home. A child who experiences kindness can develop a sense of trust and hope, leading to significant changes in their behavior and outlook on life. Kindness can show them they are valued and loved, which can help them grow into confident, compassionate adults.

Similarly, in the case of unfavorable behaviors from a mate, kindness can be a powerful force in transforming the relationship. When one partner chooses to show kindness, it can soften the heart of the other and lead to reconciliation and healing. Kindness can also help to break down walls and establish trust, leading to a deeper and more fulfilling relationship.

Kindness can be a game-changer in a toxic work environment. When coworkers show kindness to one another, it can create a positive atmosphere that fosters collaboration, productivity, and job satisfaction. Kindness can help defuse tension, reduce stress, and develop a sense of community in the workplace.

The need for kindness and love to work hand in hand is crucial in our society. We live in a world often divided by hate, fear, and mistrust. But when we show kindness and love to one another, we can break down these barriers and create a more harmonious and peaceful world. Kindness and love can unite us, inspire us, and help us to see the humanity in one another. The Bible teaches the importance of kindness and compassion. Colossians 3:12 says, "Therefore, as God's chosen people, holy and dearly loved, clothe yourselves with compassion, kindness, humility, gentleness, and patience." And Ephesians 4:32 says, "Be kind and compassionate to one another, forgiving each other, just as in Christ God forgave you." In conclusion, let us cultivate kindness, compassion, and empathy daily and be agents of healing and love in our families, communities, and world.

Transformative Questions to Ponder:

1. Reflecting on instances where you've experienced kindness, how has it impacted your outlook on life and your interactions with others? Consider how practicing kindness, compassion, and empathy can create ripple effects of positivity in your life and those around you.

   _____
   _____
   _____
   _____
   _____
   _____
   _____

2. Think about a relationship or situation in which kindness significantly transformed dynamics or resolved conflict. What lessons can you draw from that experience, and how can you intentionally incorporate kindness into your interactions to foster healing and reconciliation?

   _____
   _____
   _____
   _____
   _____
   _____
   _____

3. Considering the current state of the world, characterized by division and mistrust, how can acts of kindness and love serve as catalysts for unity and understanding? Reflect on ways you can contribute to creating a more harmonious and compassionate society by embodying the virtues of kindness, compassion, and empathy in your daily life.

_____
_____
_____
_____
_____
_____
_____

The Humility Imperative: Counteracting the 'Me-First' Mentality

We reside in a culture that prioritizes self-interest above all else, often neglecting the needs of others in favor of our desires. But how did this "me-first" effect spiral out of control? While seemingly complex, the answer ultimately boils down to a lack of humility.

This pervasive "me-first" mentality has permeated various aspects of our lives, influencing how we navigate marital relationships, parental responsibilities, personal accountability, and economic support for others.

Focusing on self-interest in marital relationships can lead to conflict, resentment, and a communication breakdown. When both partners prioritize their own needs above the needs of their spouse, it creates an environment of competition rather than collaboration. However, humility allows couples to prioritize their partner's well-being, fostering mutual respect, understanding, and compromise.

> Ephesians 5:21 (NIV) - "Submit to one another out of reverence for Christ."

Parental responsibilities are also affected by the "me-first" mentality, as parents may prioritize their desires or interests over the needs of their children. This can lead to neglect, emotional distance, and a lack of support for the child's growth and development. Humility in parenting involves putting aside personal desires and ego to prioritize the well-being and nurturing of the child.

> Philippians 2:3-4 (NIV) - "Do nothing out of selfish ambition or vain conceit. Rather, in humility, value others above yourselves, not looking to your interests but each of you to the interests of the others."

Regarding personal accountability, the "me-first" mentality can manifest as a lack of responsibility for one's actions or a refusal to acknowledge the impact of one's behavior on others. Humility involves owning up to mistakes, seeking forgiveness, and making amends, even when uncomfortable or humbling.

> James 4:6 (NIV) - "But he gives us more grace. That is why Scripture says: 'God opposes the proud but shows favor to the humble.'"

Finally, in economic roles dedicated to supporting others, such as in the workplace or through charitable giving, the "me-first" mentality can lead to greed, exploitation, and inequality. Humility in economic stewardship involves recognizing our responsibility to care for the needs of others, especially the less fortunate, and using our resources wisely and compassionately.

> 1 Timothy 6:17-19 (NIV) - "Command those who are rich in this world not to be arrogant nor to put their hope in wealth, which is so uncertain, but to put their hope in God, who richly provides us with everything for our enjoyment. Command them to do good, to be rich in good deeds, and to be generous and willing to share. In this way, they will lay up treasure for themselves as a firm foundation for the coming age so that they may take hold of the life that is truly life."

In summary, the "me-first" mentality affects various aspects of our lives, but humility offers a counterbalance by promoting selflessness, compassion, and empathy. By embracing humility, we can cultivate healthier relationships, fulfill our responsibilities with integrity, and contribute to a more just and equitable society.

Unfortunately, humility has been misconstrued as a sign of weakness, a lack of confidence, or diminished self-esteem. Instead of embracing humility, the world encourages individuals to boast about their accomplishments and possessions, falsely suggesting that recognition and significance are contingent on self-promotion. This emphasis on pride, the epitome of the "me-first" effect, stands in stark opposition to humility, a virtue God values greatly, as articulated in Proverbs 16:5 and Proverbs 16:18.

> Proverbs 16:5 (NIV) - "The Lord detests all the proud of heart. Be sure of this: They will not go unpunished."

> Proverbs 16:18 (NIV) - "Pride goes before destruction, a haughty spirit before a fall."

Contrary to popular belief, humility is not a weakness but a symbol of strength. Humble individuals can recognize the merits of others and willingly give credit where it is due. Embracing humility facilitates success in various spheres of life, fostering healthier relationships at home, work, and within the community. It diminishes feelings of jealousy and self-pity, promoting harmony and cooperation with others. Moreover, humility fosters personal growth by fostering self-awareness of one's weaknesses and a willingness to improve.

Therefore, I challenge you to reassess your perception of humility. As Christians, humility is not merely a desirable trait but an essential one. Without humility, we cannot authentically demonstrate compassion and empathy toward others. Humility allows us to extend grace and understanding to all we encounter, fostering a culture of kindness and mutual respect.

Transformative Questions To Ponder:

1. Reflecting on your own experiences, how has the pervasive "me-first" mentality impacted your relationships, whether in marriage, parenting, accountability, or economic stewardship? Consider specific instances where humility could have served as a counterbalance to self-interest and improved the dynamics of these relationships.

   _____
   _____
   _____
   _____
   _____
   _____

2. In light of the scriptural passages highlighting the harmfulness of pride and the virtues of humility, how can you actively cultivate humility in your daily life? What realistic steps can you take to shift away from self-promotion and prioritize the well-being of others, both in your interactions and broader societal contexts?

   _____
   _____
   _____
   _____
   _____
   _____
   _____

3. Imagine a world where humility prevailed over pride and self-interest. How might this transform our communities, workplaces, and relationships? Reflect on the potential ripple effects of embracing humility on fostering cooperation, compassion, and equity in society, and consider how you can contribute to this vision through your actions and attitudes.

_____
_____
_____
_____
_____
_____
_____

Selflessness:
Sacrificing for the Well-Being of Others.

The invasion of selfishness has created blindness to the mindset of selflessness. For those 50 years or older, sacrificing for the well-being of others was a way of life when our parents raised us. Within our neighborhoods, if the neighbor ran short on an ingredient for a recipe, the neighbor would provide it. If a family was lacking in any essential area, neighbors provided what was lacking. That era focused on complimenting one another, not competing against one another. Unfortunately, this generation thinks giving is strange without charging interest. They believe it is weak to neglect a leisurely personal project to help another person complete a more pertinent project. We are programmed via social media and norms to focus on me first. Sacrifice is a curse word to this generation. Placing others' needs above their own is not even a thought.

Unfortunately, selflessness has not received its due respect. As a result, many have yet to tap into its power. If you have not tapped into selflessness, you can not love effectively. Thích Nhất Hạnh supports the importance of selflessness as he states, "If your love is only a will to possess, it's not love." Do you want better relationships in your life? Practice selflessness. Do you want to experience true happiness and live a fulfilled life? Practice selflessness. Matthew 20:28 (ESV) reminds us that serving others exemplifies our Christlikeness in love and actions: "For even the Son of Man came not to be served but to serve, and to give his life as a ransom for many." This is where we stop and pray, Father; please help me to have the mind of Christ so I can live a life of selflessness in your son Jesus' Name. I can only speak for myself; I am selfish. I must have his help to live this life.

Paul was talking directly to me when he wrote Philippians 2:3-4 (ESV): "Do nothing from selfish ambition or conceit but in humility count others more significant than yourselves. Let each of you look not only to his own interests but also to the interests of others." Let's pray once more. Father, I need your help; I have been programmed from birth to be selfish and to put what I want above others, so please change my mindset from a me-first mentality to others first, in Jesus' Name.

Although our world wants us to continue to believe that selflessness is weakness, God has shown us through his Son Jesus that it is powerful! Let's explore its power by first understanding what it means to be selfless.

Selflessness means intentionally serving others even when it is not requested or appreciated. It means serving your enemy or those who do not look or carry themselves as you would carry yourself. Now that we understand selflessness, let's explore the four personal powers you ignite when you live selflessly.

The four powers of selflessness — empathy and understanding, inner peace and fulfillment, resilience and strength, and influence and inspiration — are crucial attributes that enrich our lives and reflect the love and selflessness demonstrated by Jesus Christ.

1. **Empathy and Understanding:** Jesus epitomized empathy and understanding throughout His ministry. He showed compassion for the marginalized, the sick, and the sinners, understanding their struggles and offering them hope and healing. Matthew 9:36 says, "When he saw the crowds, he had compassion for them, because they were harassed and helpless, like sheep without a shepherd."

2. **Inner Peace and Fulfillment:** Jesus found inner peace and fulfillment in fulfilling His Father's will and serving others. Despite facing immense challenges and persecution, His unwavering commitment to love and sacrifice brought Him a profound sense of peace. He said in John 14:27, "Peace I leave with you; my peace I give you. I do not give to you as the world gives. Do not let your hearts be troubled, and do not be afraid."

3. **Resilience and Strength:** Jesus displayed unparalleled resilience and strength in His journey to the cross. Despite experiencing agony and temptation in the Garden of Gethsemane, He willingly submitted to God's plan, demonstrating extraordinary

strength of character. Hebrews 12:2 states, "For the joy set before him he endured the cross, scorning its shame, and sat down at the right hand of the throne of God."

4. **Influence and Inspiration:** Jesus' selfless life and sacrificial love continue to inspire countless people worldwide. His teachings and example have shaped cultures, transformed lives, and inspired generations to love and serve others. As followers of Christ, we are called to emulate His example and share His love with others. In Matthew 5:16, Jesus says, "In the same way, let your light shine before others, that they may see your good deeds and glorify your Father in heaven."

In summary, the powers of selflessness reflect the love Jesus demonstrated through His life, teachings, and ultimate sacrifice on the cross. By embodying empathy, inner peace, resilience, and influence, we must follow in His footsteps and continue His mission of love and redemption.

Transformative Questions To Ponder:

1. What values and beliefs have shaped my understanding of selflessness, and how do they compare to today's societal norms? Reflecting on the contrast between the values instilled in previous generations, when selflessness was a way of life, and the prevalent attitudes of today's society, where self-centeredness often prevails, can prompt introspection about personal values and priorities.

   _____
   _____
   _____
   _____
   _____
   _____

2. In what ways do I prioritize self-interest over serving others, and how does this impact my relationships and overall well-being? Examining instances where self-interest precedes opportunities to serve others can reveal behavior and thought patterns that may hinder personal growth and fulfillment.

   _____
   _____
   _____
   _____
   _____
   _____

3. How can I cultivate a mindset of selflessness in my daily life, drawing inspiration from Jesus Christ's example and the teachings of scripture? Exploring practical steps to integrate selfless attitudes and actions into daily routines, such as prioritizing the needs of others, practicing empathy, and seeking opportunities to serve, can foster personal growth and alignment with values rooted in love and compassion.

_____
_____
_____
_____
_____
_____
_____

Forgiveness:
Letting go of Resentment and Extending Grace.

Forgiveness is a profound act that releases us from resentment and opens the door to grace. It's understandable if forgiveness feels elusive in a culture that often glorifies holding onto grudges. Yet, harboring unforgiveness takes a toll, affecting us mentally, physically, spiritually, and even financially.

Consider the extraordinary example of Jesus Christ, who embodied forgiveness in its purest form. Despite enduring unimaginable cruelty and betrayal, he forgave his persecutors even as he suffered on the cross. In Luke 23:34, amid agony and humiliation, Jesus uttered the profound words, "Father, forgive them, for they know not what they do." This act of mercy exemplifies the transformative power of forgiveness, even in the face of profound injustice.

Reflecting on Christ's example inspires us to extend forgiveness and grace to others, regardless of their wrongdoing. It's crucial to understand that forgiveness does not negate the pain or injustice we've experienced. Instead, it frees from the chains of bitterness and resentment, creating the way for healing.

When grappling with forgiveness, it's essential to acknowledge our own humanity. Each of us has caused pain or made mistakes at some point. Yet, despite our flaws, Jesus offered forgiveness to all. This reminder emphasizes the universal nature of forgiveness and its profound impact.

In Matthew 6:14-15, Jesus teaches about the reciprocal nature of forgiveness. He urges us to forgive others so that we may also receive forgiveness from our heavenly Father. Refusing to forgive harms us and impedes our ability to receive divine grace.

Ultimately, forgiveness is a choice to relinquish resentment and extend forgiveness and grace to those who wronged us. By embracing forgiveness, we honor Christ's example and experience liberation from releasing the weight of unforgiveness.

As I've mentioned, I understand the challenge of letting go of unforgiveness in a world that often encourages it. However, I implore you to release it. Your unforgiveness is detrimental, corroding your well-being. By refusing to forgive, you risk forfeiting God's forgiveness. Let me allow you to read the scripture for yourself: Matthew 6:14-15

> "For if you forgive others their trespasses, your heavenly Father will also forgive you, but if you do not forgive others their trespasses, neither will your Father forgive your trespasses."

Transformative Questions to Ponder:

1. How does the societal glorification of holding grudges affect my own willingness to extend forgiveness, and what steps must I take to challenge and overcome this influence in my life?

   _____
   _____
   _____
   _____
   _____
   _____
   _____
   _____

2. Reflecting on Jesus Christ's example of forgiveness on the cross, how can I embody a spirit of forgiveness even in the face of profound injustice or betrayal in my own life?

   _____
   _____
   _____
   _____
   _____
   _____
   _____
   _____

3. Considering the reciprocal nature of forgiveness taught by Jesus in Matthew 6:14-15, what are the personal implications of withholding forgiveness regarding my relationship with others and my spiritual well-being?

_____
_____
_____
_____
_____
_____
_____
_____

Perseverance:
Remaining Steadfast In Love Despite Challenges.

In the grand tapestry of life, adversity often weaves itself as formidable threads, intertwining within the intricate fabric of our relationships, workplaces, and communities. Yet, amidst the complexities of these challenges lies a transformative power—a beacon of love that transcends circumstance and propels us toward resilience. Through the unwavering lens of Christ's love, we embark on a journey of perseverance, uncovering profound truths that transcend our trials.

The first thread of our narrative unfolds within the sacred covenant of marriage. Here, amidst the ebbs and flows of human connection, couples navigate turbulent waters of financial strain, health crises, and emotional upheaval. Like intertwined vines drawing sustenance from a common source, they cling to each other with unwavering devotion, inspired by Christ's sacrificial love. Ephesians 5:25 calls them to mirror Christ's love for the church, anchoring their bond in forgiveness, support, and unyielding commitment.

Transformative Supports for Your Marriage:

Regular communication and financial planning sessions can proactively address challenges. Openly discussing financial goals, budgeting strategies, and potential stressors cultivates a shared understanding and mutual support system. Additionally, setting aside intentional time for emotional check-ins allows partners to express concerns, fears, and hopes, fostering empathy and strengthening their bond. Couples navigate financial difficulties and communication breakdowns with resilience and unity through these practices, inspired by Christ's sacrificial love.

Venturing into the realm of the workplace, we encounter another facet of our journey—where colleagues and partners traverse landscapes fraught with setbacks, conflicts, and ethical quandaries. Yet, guided by Christ's example, they navigate these challenges with integrity and humility. In Colossians 3:23-24, they find solace, realizing their labor is not in vain when dedicated to serving a higher purpose. With hearts aligned to the divine call, they cultivate a culture of trust, fostering resilience amidst adversity.

Transformative Supports for Your Workplace:

Fostering a culture of transparency and accountability within the workplace encourages open dialogue and constructive feedback channels to address conflicts and ethical dilemmas promptly. By upholding honesty, humility, and integrity in all interactions, colleagues and business partners build trust and cultivate a supportive environment. Embracing the ethos of Colossians 3:23-24, where work is viewed as service to a higher purpose, individuals align their actions with principles of Christ-like love, promoting collaboration and resilience amidst challenges.

As we widen the aperture to encompass the broader community, the final thread of our narrative emerges—a tapestry woven with the threads of social justice, compassion, and collective action. Here, individuals confronted with the specter of injustice and calamity draw inspiration from Galatians 6:9. With tireless resolve, they sow seeds of kindness, advocate for the marginalized, and extend hands of solidarity to those in need. They become beacons of hope in the crucible of adversity, illuminating the path toward a brighter tomorrow.

Transformative Supports for Your Community Interactions:

Engaging in collective acts of service and advocacy addresses social injustices and supports those affected by discrimination or natural disasters. To demonstrate compassion and solidarity, organize community initiatives such as food drives, fundraisers, or volunteer projects. By actively participating in efforts to uplift the marginalized and alleviate suffering, individuals embody the spirit of Galatians 6:9, persevering in doing good even in the face of adversity. Through these transformative actions, communities forge empathy, resilience, and unity bonds, transcending barriers and fostering positive change.

Through these interconnected threads of love, we embark on a transformative journey where challenges cease to be obstacles and instead become opportunities for growth, compassion, and profound connection. In the crucible of adversity, we discover the enduring truth that love, as demonstrated by Christ, is the steadfast anchor that sustains us through the storms of life.

Transformative Questions to Ponder:

1. How can I embody Christ's sacrificial love in my marriage, workplace, and community interactions, especially when faced with adversity? How might this transform my approach to challenges and strengthen my relationships with others?

   _____
   _____
   _____
   _____
   _____
   _____
   _____
   _____

2. How can my spouse and I proactively address challenges in our marriage, drawing inspiration from Christ's example of love and commitment? How might implementing regular communication and financial planning sessions strengthen our bond and resilience in the face of adversity?

   _____
   _____
   _____
   _____
   _____
   _____
   _____
   _____

3. How must I contribute to fostering a culture of compassion and solidarity in my community, guided by Christ-like love and social justice? What collective acts of service and advocacy can I engage in to uplift the marginalized and inspire positive change, aligning with the spirit of Galatians 6:9?

_____
_____
_____
_____
_____
_____
_____
_____

LOVE IN ACTION: PRACTICING UNCONDITIONAL LOVE

Love's Revolution: Transforming Every Aspect of Life with a Mindset of Compassion:

Chapter 3
Love in Action: Practicing Unconditional Love

Welcome to a journey of love in action. This chapter explores how unconditional love can shape our daily interactions and relationships, drawing inspiration from verses 4-7. Through examples and practical strategies, we'll discover how to embody love in all aspects of life, fostering empathy, compassion, and deeper connections. Join us as we embrace the transformative power of love and cultivate a mindset rooted in boundless compassion.

Applying Love In Various Situations and Relationships (Verses 4-7).

Patience with Family

When we choose patience and understanding in our interactions with family members, we acknowledge their imperfections and embrace them with empathy and compassion. Refraining from reacting impulsively to their shortcomings creates a space for mutual growth and acceptance within the family dynamic. This patience allows us to see beyond momentary frustrations and invest in long-term relationships built on trust and unconditional love.

> Scripture: Colossians 3:13 - "Bear with each other and forgive one another if any of you has a grievance against someone. Forgive as the Lord forgave you."

Forgiveness in Conflict

Conflict is inevitable in any relationship, but how we respond can make all the difference. By practicing forgiveness instead of holding onto grudges, we release the burden of past hurts and pave the way for reconciliation and healing. Letting go of resentment allows us to approach conflicts with a fresh perspective and a willingness to find common ground. In doing so, we foster an environment of understanding and empathy, strengthening the bonds of friendship and camaraderie.

> Ephesians 4:32: "Be kind and compassionate to one another, forgiving each other, just as in Christ God forgave you."

Generosity towards Strangers

In a world characterized by self-interest, generosity towards strangers is a powerful reminder of our interconnectedness and shared humanity. We embody unconditional love when we extend kindness without expecting anything in return. Whether offering a helping hand to someone in need or simply showing compassion to a stranger, these gestures can brighten someone's day and inspire others to pay it forward. Our actions contribute to creating a more compassionate and inclusive society.

> Scripture: Hebrews 13:16 - "And do not forget to do good and to share with others, for with such sacrifices God is pleased."

Empathy in Listening

Genuine empathy goes beyond mere listening; it involves intentionally seeking to understand and validate the experiences of others. When we approach conversations with an open heart and a willingness to empathize, we create a sacred space for individuals to express themselves authentically. We foster deeper connections and cultivate mutual respect by acknowledging feelings and perspectives without judgment. This empathetic listening strengthens our relationships and allows us to learn and grow from the diverse experiences of those around us.

> James 1:19: "My dear brothers and sisters, take note of this: Everyone should be quick to listen, slow to speak, and slow to become angry."

Transformative Questions to Ponder:

1. How can I cultivate a more profound sense of patience and understanding in my interactions with family members, especially during frustration or disagreement? How can I approach these situations with empathy and compassion, fostering stronger bonds and nurturing a more harmonious family dynamic?

   _____
   _____
   _____
   _____
   _____

2. What barriers or obstacles prevent me from forgiving and letting go of past grievances in my relationships? How might practicing forgiveness contribute to more incredible emotional healing and reconciliation, allowing for deeper connections and mutual growth? What strategies can I employ to cultivate a mindset of forgiveness and compassion in conflict?

   _____
   _____
   _____
   _____
   _____

3. **Considering Generosity towards Strangers:** How can I incorporate generosity and kindness into my daily life, particularly towards those I encounter who may be in need? How might these small gestures of compassion foster a more inclusive and compassionate community, fostering a sense of interconnectedness and shared humanity? How can I challenge myself to extend kindness without expectation, embodying the principles of unconditional love in my interactions with strangers and acquaintances?

_____
_____
_____
_____
_____
_____
_____
_____

Love Unveiled:
Everyday Encounters Illuminating Acts of Kindness

Small Acts of Kindness: Our most minor acts of kindness can significantly impact others' lives in our daily interactions. By embracing opportunities to spread love through simple gestures, we contribute to a more compassionate and interconnected world where kindness is the currency of human connection.

Examples: Holding the door open for someone, offering a genuine compliment, or helping a neighbor carry their groceries are all simple yet powerful demonstrations of love. These acts of kindness will brighten someone's day and foster a sense of community connection and belonging.

Active Listening: True listening is an act of love that requires us to set aside our agendas and be fully present for others. Engaging in active listening creates space for deeper understanding and empathy, fostering stronger bonds and nurturing authentic connections in our relationships.

Examples: Listening attentively to a friend or family member without interrupting or rushing to offer advice demonstrates love and respect for their thoughts and feelings. By showing empathy and validation through active listening, we create space for meaningful communication and deepen our relationships.

Expressing Gratitude: Gratitude is a language of love that transcends words. It expresses appreciation for the abundance in our lives and the kindness of others. By cultivating gratitude in our daily interactions, we foster a culture of appreciation and reciprocity where love flows freely and abundantly.

Examples: Saying "thank you" to the cashier at the grocery store, sending a handwritten note of appreciation to a coworker, or expressing gratitude to loved ones for their support are all ways to cultivate love in our daily interactions. Practicing gratitude fosters a sense of abundance and strengthens our connections with others.

Offering Support: Offering support to others in need is a tangible expression of love and solidarity. When we extend a helping hand or a listening ear to struggling people, we affirm their worth and remind them that they are not alone in their journey. Doing so strengthens our connections and creates a community built on compassion and mutual care.

Examples: Whether it's lending a listening ear to a friend in need, providing emotional support during a difficult time, or offering practical assistance with a task or project, showing up for others in times of need is a powerful expression of love. We demonstrate our commitment to caring for and uplifting those around us by providing support.

Acts of Service: Service is love made visible, embodying our commitment to caring for others and making a positive difference in the world. When we engage in acts of service, we demonstrate our capacity for empathy and selflessness, enriching our lives and the lives of those around us with the transformative power of love in action.

Examples: Volunteering in our communities, helping a family member with chores or errands, or cooking a meal for a friend feeling overwhelmed are all examples of love in action through acts of service. These selfless gestures demonstrate our willingness to put others' needs before our own and contribute to the well-being of our communities.

Transformative Questions to Ponder:

1. How can I become more attuned to small acts of kindness daily, and how might embracing these opportunities contribute to a more profound sense of connection and belonging within my community?

2. What barriers or distractions hinder my ability to engage in active listening, and how can I cultivate a mindset of presence and empathy to nurture more authentic connections in my relationships?

3. How can I cultivate gratitude in my daily interactions, and how might expressing appreciation contribute to a culture of reciprocity and abundance in my personal and professional spheres?

_____
_____
_____
_____
_____
_____
_____

Love's Revolution:
Transforming Every Aspect of Life with a Mindset of Compassion

Cultivating a mindset of love in all aspects of life is a transformative journey that requires intentional effort and continuous practice. To truly embrace love as a guiding principle, we can focus on several key areas:

Self-Love:

Start by cultivating a deep sense of love and acceptance for oneself, as commanded in Scripture: "Love your neighbor as yourself" (Mark 12:31). This involves embracing our strengths and weaknesses, recognizing that we are fearfully and wonderfully made by God (Psalm 139:14). Practicing self-compassion allows us to extend the same grace and understanding to ourselves that we offer to others, understanding that we are imperfect beings in need of love and forgiveness.

By prioritizing self-care, we honor the temple of the Holy Spirit within us (1 Corinthians 6:19-20). This may include setting boundaries to protect our physical, emotional, and spiritual well-being, engaging in activities that nourish our souls, and seeking rest and renewal in God's presence. By cultivating a positive self-image rooted in God's unconditional love for us, we lay the foundation for extending that love to others.

As we learn to love ourselves as God loves us, we become better equipped to love our neighbors with the same depth and sincerity. Our ability to show others compassion, empathy, and kindness is intimately connected to our love for ourselves. By recognizing and affirming our worth, we create a reservoir of love from which we can freely give to others, fulfilling the greatest commandment to love our neighbors as ourselves.

Embracing our Worth

We should recognize and appreciate our inherent worth as individuals created in God's image (Genesis 1:27). Understanding that we are loved unconditionally by a higher power can strengthen our self-worth.

Practicing Self-Compassion

We must show ourselves the same kindness and understanding we extend to others. This involves forgiving ourselves for past mistakes and embracing our imperfections with grace.

Prioritizing Self-Care

We must intentionally care for our physical, emotional, and spiritual well-being. This should include engaging in activities that bring us joy, setting boundaries to protect our time and energy, and seeking support when needed.

Interpersonal Relationships

Interpersonal relationships are the precious garments woven with threads of love, empathy, and understanding in our lives. As followers of Christ, we are called to foster loving connections with those around us, mirroring the love that God has shown us. Scripture teaches us to "love one another deeply, from the heart" (1 Peter 1:22), extending this love to our family, friends, colleagues, and acquaintances.

Active Listening

Active listening becomes a sacred practice, allowing us to hear the words spoken and the heart behind them. James 1:19 reminds us, "Let every person be quick to hear, slow to speak, slow to anger." Through empathetic listening, we enter into the experiences of others, sharing in their joys and sorrows.

Forgiveness

Forgiveness is a cornerstone of healthy relationships, reflecting the forgiveness we have received through Christ's sacrifice. Colossians 3:13 urges us to "bear with each other and forgive one another if any of you has a grievance against someone. Forgive as the Lord forgave you." We pave the way for reconciliation and healing by releasing grudges and extending grace.

Communication

Communication serves as the lifeblood of relationships, allowing us to express our thoughts, feelings, and needs honestly and clearly. Proverbs 15:1 reminds us that "a gentle answer turns away wrath, but a harsh word stirs up anger." By speaking truth in love (Ephesians 4:15), we cultivate trust and understanding in our interactions.

Genuine Compassion

Genuine compassion flows from hearts transformed by God's love, moving us to act with kindness and generosity toward others. Philippians 2:4 encourages us to "look to your interests but also to the interests of others." By considering the needs of those around us and extending a helping hand, we demonstrate Christ's love in tangible ways.

Nurturing these qualities within our interpersonal relationships creates spaces of warmth and belonging where mutual respect and care thrive. Through love, forgiveness, communication, and compassion, we build bridges that connect hearts and cultivate a community rooted in the transformative power of God's love.

Active Listening and Empathy

Practice active listening to understand others' perspectives and feelings truly. Cultivate empathy by putting ourselves in their shoes and responding compassionately (1 Peter 3:8).

Forgiveness and Reconciliation

Embrace the power of forgiveness to heal relationships and let go of resentment. We must intentionally seek reconciliation with those we have hurt or who have hurt us, extending grace as we have received grace (Ephesians 4:32).

Expressing Love Through Actions

Demonstrate love through tangible actions such as kindness, encouragement, and support. Let our words and deeds reflect the love that God has shown us (1 John 3:18).

Community and Service

Community and service are the avenues through which we express Christ's love to the world, extending beyond the confines of our immediate circles to embrace the broader community. As followers of Jesus, we are called to embody His example of selfless love and sacrificial service, reaching out to those in need and contributing to the well-being of our communities.

Scripture reminds us of our interconnectedness and the importance of loving our neighbors as ourselves. Galatians 5:13 urges us, "Serve one another humbly in love." By humbling ourselves in service, we demonstrate Christ's love in action, seeking the welfare of others above our interests.

Engaging in acts of service is not merely a duty but a joyful response to God's grace. 1 Peter 4:10 encourages us, "Each of you should use whatever gift you have received to serve others as faithful stewards of God's grace in its various forms." Whether through volunteering, supporting charitable causes, or simply being present for those in need, we can be vessels of God's love and grace in the world.

Recognizing our interconnectedness reminds us that we are all part of God's diverse and beautiful tapestry of creation. Romans 12:5 declares, "So in Christ, we, though many, form one body, and each member belongs to all the others." By showing kindness to strangers and hospitality to those outside our immediate circles, we foster a culture of compassion and solidarity, reflecting the unity and love found in Christ.

Through acts of service and expressions of kindness, we participate in God's redemptive work in the world, bringing hope, healing, and restoration to broken lives and communities. As we extend love beyond ourselves and into our communities, we become instruments of God's transformative grace, shining the light of His love in a world that needs hope and compassion.

- **Volunteering and Giving Back**: Engage in acts of service that benefit our communities and those in need. Planning to volunteer at a local shelter, participating in a community clean-up, or supporting a charitable organization, every act of service makes a difference (Galatians 6:9-10).
- **Building Meaningful Connections**: Foster genuine connections with people from diverse backgrounds and experiences. Seek to understand and appreciate each individual's unique contributions, recognizing the inherent value in every person (Romans 12:10).
- **Promoting Unity and Cooperation**: Work towards building a sense of unity and cooperation within our communities. Be a peacemaker and bridge builder, striving to resolve conflicts and promote harmony among neighbors and fellow citizens (Matthew 5:9).

Global Perspective

Embracing a global perspective rooted in love requires us to transcend boundaries and embrace the rich tapestry of humanity that God has created. Scripture calls us to love our neighbors as ourselves, extending compassion and understanding to all people regardless of their background or beliefs (Matthew 22:39). By cultivating empathy and seeking to understand diverse cultures, perspectives, and experiences, we embody the love of Christ in a world often divided by fear and prejudice.

Challenging prejudices is essential to building a more just and equitable society. James 2:9 reminds us, "But if you show favoritism, you sin and are convicted by the law as lawbreakers." By confronting bias and discrimination, we witness the transformative power of love, breaking down barriers that separate us from one another and inhibiting the full expression of God's kingdom on earth.

Advocating for social justice is a natural outgrowth of our commitment to love and serve others. Isaiah 1:17 implores us, "Learn to do right; seek justice. Defend the oppressed. Take up the fatherless's cause; plead the widow's case." By standing up for the marginalized and oppressed, we align ourselves with God's heart for the vulnerable and contribute to realizing His kingdom, where justice flows like a mighty river.

Promoting inclusivity and equality requires intentional effort and a willingness to challenge systems of oppression and privilege. Galatians 3:28 proclaims, "There is neither Jew nor Gentile, neither slave nor free, nor is there male and female, for you are all one in Christ Jesus." By recognizing our shared humanity and working towards a more just and equitable world, we witness the transformative power of love to heal divisions and reconcile all things to God.

In embracing a global perspective rooted in love, we become agents of positive change in a world hungry for compassion and understanding. By recognizing the dignity and worth of every individual and working towards a more just and equitable world, we participate in God's redemptive work, gracefully and liberally providing hope, healing, and reconciliation to a broken and divided world.

- **Advocating for Justice and Equality:** Stand up for the rights and dignity of all people, especially those marginalized or oppressed. Speak out against injustice and work towards creating a more equitable and inclusive society (Micah 6:8).
- **Cultivating Cross-Cultural Understanding:** Seek to learn from and appreciate the diversity of cultures, beliefs, and perspectives worldwide. Embrace opportunities to engage with people from different backgrounds, recognizing that our differences enrich the human experience (Revelation 7:9-10).

- **Praying for Peace and Healing:** Lift up prayers for peace, reconciliation, and healing in our world. Ask God to guide us in becoming instruments of His love and grace, bringing hope and restoration to broken communities and nations (Philippians 4:6-7).

In each of these areas, cultivating a mindset of love requires deliberate intentionality and a willingness to align our thoughts and actions with the teachings of love in Scripture. By embodying the principles of unconditional love in our daily lives, we experience personal transformation and contribute to the realization of God's kingdom of love on earth

Transformative Questions to Ponder:

1. How can I practice self-compassion and prioritize self-care in alignment with Scripture's command to "love your neighbor as yourself" (Mark 12:31), recognizing that caring for myself equips me to extend love to others better?

   _____
   _____
   _____
   _____
   _____
   _____
   _____
   _____

2. In my interpersonal relationships, how can I embody the qualities of active listening, forgiveness, and genuine compassion as outlined in Scripture (James 1:19, Colossians 3:13, Philippians 2:4), fostering deeper connections and harmony with those around me?

   _____
   _____
   _____
   _____
   _____
   _____
   _____
   _____

3. When engaging with the global community, how can I cultivate empathy, advocate for justice and equality, and promote inclusivity and understanding across diverse cultures and perspectives, guided by Scripture's call to love our neighbors and seek justice (Matthew 22:39, Isaiah 1:17, Galatians 3:28)?

_____
_____
_____
_____
_____
_____
_____
_____

OVERCOMING OBSTACLES TO LOVE

Practicing forgiveness and reconciliation in relationships:

Chapter 4
Overcoming Obstacles to Love

Overcoming obstacles to love is a journey of self-awareness and growth, guided by the timeless wisdom of 1 Corinthians 13:5. This scripture teaches us that love is not easily angered and keeps no record of wrongs. By embracing this truth, we learn to recognize and address the barriers that hinder the expression of love in our lives, such as anger, resentment, and unforgiveness. We can navigate these obstacles through intentional self-reflection, humility, and grace, paving the way for deeper connections and restored relationships. As we embody the transformative power of love, we experience healing, reconciliation, and the fullness of God's intended purpose for our lives.

Identifying and Addressing Obstacles to Love (Verse 5).

In our journey of love, we often encounter obstacles that hinder its expression and growth. We must identify and address these barriers to experience the fullness of love as intended by God. As the Apostle Paul writes in 1 Corinthians 13:5, "Love... is not easily angered, it keeps no record of wrongs." This scripture underscores the importance of recognizing and dealing with emotions and attitudes obstructing love, such as anger, resentment, and grudges. By acknowledging these obstacles and seeking guidance from God's Word, we can cultivate a patient, kind, and enduring love.

1. **Practicing Self-Reflection:** Reflect on your emotions and attitudes, especially during conflict or relationship tension. Psalm 139:23-24 encourages this practice: "Search me, God, and know my heart; test me and know my anxious thoughts. See if there is any offensive way in me, and lead me in the way everlasting." We can actively address and overcome obstacles by inviting God to search our hearts and reveal any hindrances to love.

2. **Seeking Accountability and Feedback:** Surround yourself with trustworthy individuals who can provide honest feedback and accountability in areas where obstacles to love may exist. Proverbs 27:6 says, "Wounds from a friend can be trusted, but an enemy multiplies kisses." Engaging in open and transparent dialogue with others allows for growth and transformation, as constructive criticism can illuminate blind spots and encourage positive change.

Understanding the Role of Anger and Resentment in Hindering Love:

Anger and resentment can be significant barriers to experiencing and expressing love in our relationships. Ephesians 4:26-27 advises, "In your anger do not sin: Do not let the sun go down while you are still angry, and do not give the devil a foothold." This passage highlights the potential destructive power of unchecked anger and its ability to disrupt the harmony of relationships. By understanding the role of anger and resentment and their negative impact on love, we can begin the journey of healing and restoration, allowing God's transformative love to permeate our hearts and relationships.

1. **Practicing Anger Management Techniques:** Learn and implement healthy ways to manage anger and resentment, such as deep breathing, taking a timeout, or expressing emotions through journaling or exercise. James 1:19-20 advises, "My dear brothers and sisters, take note of this: Everyone should be quick to listen, slow to speak and become angry because our anger does not produce the righteousness that God desires." By intentionally responding to situations with patience and self-control, we can prevent anger from escalating and hindering love.

2. **Seeking Professional Help:** If anger and resentment persist despite efforts to manage them independently, seek guidance from a qualified counselor or therapist. Proverbs 11:14 states, "For lack of guidance a nation falls, but victory is won through many advisers." Professional support can offer valuable insights and strategies tailored to individual circumstances, facilitating relationship healing and restoration.

Strategies For Managing and Overcoming Negative Emotions:

God equips us with strategies for managing and overcoming negative emotions that threaten to overshadow love. Philippians 4:6-7 encourages us, "Do not be anxious about anything, but in every situation, by prayer and petition, with thanksgiving, present your requests to God. And the peace of God, which transcends all understanding, will guard your hearts and minds in Christ Jesus." Through prayer, gratitude, and seeking God's peace, we can navigate challenging emotions and find the strength to overcome them. Additionally, seeking support from trusted mentors or counselors can provide valuable guidance and perspective in managing negative emotions.

1. **Practicing Gratitude and Positive Affirmations:** Cultivate gratitude by regularly expressing thankfulness for big and small blessings. Philippians 4:8 encourages this mindset: "Finally, brothers and sisters, whatever is true, whatever is noble, whatever is right, whatever is pure, whatever is lovely, whatever is admirable—if anything is excellent or praiseworthy—think about such things." Focusing on positive aspects of life can counteract negative emotions and foster a sense of peace and contentment.

2. **Engaging in Emotional Release Activities:** Explore healthy outlets for releasing pent-up emotions, such as journaling, creative expression, or physical activity. Ecclesiastes 3:4 acknowledges the seasonality of emotions: "A time to weep and a time to laugh, a time to mourn and a time to dance." By accepting and processing emotions constructively, we can prevent them from festering and overwhelming our hearts and minds.

Practicing Forgiveness and Reconciliation in Relationships:

Forgiveness and reconciliation are essential aspects of cultivating love in our relationships. Colossians 3:13 urges, "Bear with each other and forgive one another if any of you has a grievance against someone. Forgive as the Lord forgave you." Embracing the example set by Christ's sacrificial love, we are called to extend forgiveness and pursue reconciliation, even in the face of hurt and betrayal. Through humility, grace, and the power of God's love, we can heal wounds, restore broken relationships, and experience the transformative impact of forgiveness in our lives.

1. **Embracing Humility and Grace:** One transformative strategy for practicing forgiveness and reconciliation is cultivating a spirit of humility and grace, following the example set by Christ. Philippians 2:3-4 advises, "Do nothing out of selfish ambition or vain conceit. Rather, in humility, value others above yourselves, not looking to your interests but each of you to the interests of the others." By prioritizing the well-being and restoration of relationships over personal pride or vindication, we open the door to reconciliation and healing. Ephesians 4:32 reinforces this approach, urging us to "Be kind and compassionate to one another, forgiving each other, just as in Christ God forgave you."

2. **Initiating Honest and Vulnerable Communication:** Another transformative strategy is to initiate honest and vulnerable communication with the person we must forgive or reconcile with. Matthew 18:15 provides a framework for this process: "If your brother or sister sins, go and point out their fault, just between the two of you. If they listen to you, you have won them over." By approaching the individual in a spirit of love and humility, we create space for dialogue, understanding, and reconciliation. James 5:16 also encourages us to "Confess your sins to each other and pray for each other so that you may be healed." Opening up about our faults and shortcomings can foster empathy and pave the way for mutual forgiveness and relationship restoration.

These strategies, supported by Scripture, provide practical guidance for overcoming obstacles to love and fostering healthier, more fulfilling relationships.

Transformative Questions to Ponder:

1. How can I cultivate a spirit of humility and grace, as exemplified by Christ, in my relationships to overcome obstacles to love? (Philippians 2:3-4)

_____
_____
_____
_____
_____
_____
_____
_____

2. Am I willing to initiate honest and vulnerable communication with those I must forgive or reconcile with, following the biblical principles outlined in Matthew 18:15 and James 5:16?

_____
_____
_____
_____
_____
_____
_____
_____

3. How can I actively practice gratitude and positive affirmations, as recommended in Philippians 4:8, to counteract negative emotions and foster a more profound sense of peace and contentment in my life and relationships?

_____
_____
_____
_____
_____
_____
_____
_____

THE RIPPLE EFFECT: SPREADING LOVE IN A WORLD OF HATE

Inspiring others to embrace love as a guiding principle for social change:

Chapter 5
The Ripple Effect: Spreading Love in a World of Hate

Harnessing the Transformative Power of Love's Characteristics (Verses 4-7):

In the sacred verses of 1 Corinthians 13:4-7, the essence of love is beautifully illuminated, revealing its unparalleled transformative power. Love, depicted as patient, kind, selfless, and enduring, becomes not just a sentiment but a dynamic force capable of profound change. As we embrace and embody these divine characteristics, we unlock the potential for a metamorphosis within ourselves and the world around us.

Scripture:

> 1 Corinthians 13:4-7 (NIV) - "Love is patient, love is kind. It does not envy, it does not boast, it is not proud. It does not dishonor others; it is not self-seeking; it is not easily angered; it keeps no record of wrongs. Love does not delight in evil but rejoices with the truth. It always protects, always trusts, always hopes, always perseveres."

Consider the journey of an individual grappling with anger and impatience. Through deep reflection and prayer, they resolve to embody the transformative love described in Corinthians. Over time, this commitment yields a remarkable evolution as they grow more patient, kind, and compassionate in their interactions and demeanor.

In another scenario, envision a community torn asunder by strife and discord. Here, a collective decision emerges to embrace forgiveness and reconciliation, guided by the timeless wisdom of scripture. Through acts of grace and understanding, healing takes root, and the once-fractured bonds of unity begin to mend, restoring harmony and wholeness to the community.

Transformative Questions To Ponder:

1. How can we cultivate patience and kindness in our interactions, drawing inspiration from the transformative qualities of love described in 1 Corinthians 13:4-7?

_____
_____
_____
_____
_____
_____
_____
_____
_____

2. How can we transcend our desires and egos to embody the selflessness and humility inherent in love, as outlined in the sacred verses?

_____
_____
_____
_____
_____
_____
_____
_____

3. Reflecting on the power of forgiveness and reconciliation in healing fractured communities, how might we actively promote understanding and grace in our spheres of influence, fostering unity and harmony?

_____
_____
_____
_____
_____
_____
_____
_____
_____

Creating a Ripple Effect of Positivity and Kindness:

In the symphony of life, acts of kindness and positivity resonate as powerful notes, creating a harmonious ripple effect that echoes far beyond their initial expression. Like a stone cast into a still pond, these gestures send forth concentric waves of goodwill, touching hearts and transforming lives throughout communities and societies. No matter how seemingly small, each act becomes a luminous beacon of hope, inspiring others to join in and propagate a virtuous cycle of benevolence.

Scripture:

> Luke 6:38 (NIV) - "Give, and it will be given to you. A good measure, pressed down, shaken together, and running over, will be poured into your lap. For with the measure you use, it will be measured to you."

Consider the narrative of a young soul who dedicates their time to serving at a local homeless shelter, offering nourishment and companionship to those in need. Witnessing the selflessness of this act, others in the community are stirred to action, amplifying the impact and spreading waves of positivity that reverberate throughout the neighborhood.

In another instance, envision a simple yet profound act of kindness—a stranger's coffee paid for, a compassionate ear lent to a distressed friend. These gestures, born from empathy and goodwill, trigger a cascade of reciprocity and compassion. Inspired by the kindness bestowed upon them, recipients are moved to pay it forward, setting a boundless current of benevolence that transcends time and space.

Transformative Questions to Ponder:

1. How can we intentionally sow seeds of kindness and positivity in our daily interactions, recognizing their potential to create a ripple effect of goodwill that extends far beyond our immediate surroundings?

   _____
   _____
   _____
   _____
   _____
   _____
   _____
   _____

2. Reflecting on the principle of reciprocity highlighted in Luke 6:38, how might we approach acts of giving and generosity with a mindset of abundance, trusting in the exponential impact they can have on fostering a culture of compassion and empathy?

   _____
   _____
   _____
   _____
   _____
   _____
   _____
   _____

3. Considering the inspiring narratives of individuals catalyzing waves of positivity through selfless acts, how can we cultivate a culture of kindness within our communities, empowering others to join in and contribute to the ongoing cycle of benevolence and upliftment?

_____
_____
_____
_____
_____
_____
_____
_____

Examining the Impact of Love On Communities and Societies

With its profound and transformative essence, love weaves its threads through the tapestry of communities and societies, shaping their ethos, actions, and relationships. As it saturates the societal fabric, love becomes the catalyst for unity, compassion, and understanding, bridging divides and fostering a sense of interconnectedness among individuals of diverse backgrounds. In communities where love reigns supreme, resilience, inclusivity, and solidarity flourish, equipping inhabitants to confront challenges with grace and fortitude.

Scripture:

> 1 John 4:11-12 (NIV) - "Dear friends, since God so loved us, we also ought to love one another. No one has ever seen God, but if we love one another, God lives in us, and his love is complete in us."

Consider the narrative of a society marred by the scars of inequality and injustice. Here, a grassroots movement fueled by the fiery flame of love and a steadfast commitment to social justice emerges as a beacon of hope. Through tireless advocacy, enlightened education, and grassroots organizing, this movement gathers momentum, effecting tangible policy reforms and ushering in transformative changes that uplift the lives of marginalized communities.

In another scenario, envisage a diverse tapestry of individuals coalescing around a common cause, such as the urgent need to address environmental degradation. Drawing upon their shared values of love and stewardship, these disparate voices harmonize in collaborative action, crafting sustainable solutions that resonate with compassion and responsibility. In this collective endeavor, love transcends barriers of difference, uniting hearts and hands to pursue the greater good.

Transformative Questions to Ponder:

1. How can we actively cultivate a culture of love within our communities and societies, recognizing its profound impact on fostering unity, compassion, and understanding among individuals from diverse backgrounds?

   _____
   _____
   _____
   _____
   _____
   _____
   _____
   _____

2. Reflecting on the narrative of grassroots movements fueled by love and commitment to social justice, how might we contribute to or initiate similar efforts within our spheres of influence, catalyzing transformative changes that uplift and empower marginalized communities?

   _____
   _____
   _____
   _____
   _____
   _____
   _____
   _____

3. Considering the collaborative action taken by individuals united by a shared concern for environmental degradation, how can we harness the power of love and stewardship to address pressing global challenges, fostering a collective sense of responsibility and compassion towards the planet and all its inhabitants?

_____
_____
_____
_____
_____
_____
_____
_____
_____

Inspiring Others to Embrace Love as a Guiding Principle of Social Change.

As we embrace love as a guiding principle for societal transformation, we become harbingers of profound change within our immediate communities and across broader horizons. Fueled by the boundless energy of love, our actions serve as beacons of inspiration, igniting a radiant cascade of positive transformation that reverberates far and wide. Love, with its transcendent power, dissolves barriers of division, uniting diverse individuals under the standard banner of compassion and justice.

Scripture:

> Matthew 5:16 (NIV) - "In the same way, let your light shine before others, that they may see your good deeds and glorify your Father in heaven."

Consider the narrative of a charismatic leader who leads by example, embodying the essence of love in every interaction and decision. Through their unwavering authenticity and integrity, they kindle the flames of inspiration in the hearts of others, catalyzing a movement steeped in the transformative power of love and compassion.

In another inspiring tale, envision a collective of young activists harnessing the creative force of art and storytelling to amplify the voices of love and solidarity within their community. Through their evocative expressions, they initiate meaningful dialogues and spark vital conversations about the pivotal role of love in propelling societal change forward.

In these examples, love emerges as the driving force behind a movement for positive societal transformation, illuminating pathways toward a more just, compassionate, and equitable world for all.

Transformative Questions to Ponder

1. How can we authentically embody the principles of love, compassion, and justice in our own lives, serving as catalysts for societal transformation and inspiring others to do the same?

   _____
   _____
   _____
   _____
   _____
   _____
   _____

2. Reflecting on the narratives of a charismatic leader and a collective of young activists, how might we leverage our unique strengths and talents to amplify the message of love and solidarity, foster meaningful dialogue, and ignite movements for positive social change?

   _____
   _____
   _____
   _____
   _____
   _____
   _____

3. Considering the profound impact of love as a guiding principle in driving societal transformation, what steps can we take to cultivate a culture of empathy, understanding, and unity within our communities, paving the way for a more inclusive and equitable world?

_____
_____
_____
_____
_____
_____
_____
_____

Survey Your Transformative Journey

Thank you for navigating through this transformative journey into the heart of love. As you reflect on the insights shared in "Love's Unconditional Revolution - Unleash the Transformative Power of Love," we invite you to ponder the following questions and consider the strategies provided to unleash the transformative power of love in your life and beyond:

1. What does it mean to love others, as outlined in 1 Corinthians 13:4-7? Reflect on the qualities of love described in these verses—patience, kindness, humility, selflessness, forgiveness, and perseverance—and consider how you can embody these qualities in your interactions and relationships.

2. How can you cultivate a deeper understanding of love's essence and its transformative power? Explore the teachings of 1 Corinthians 13 and other scriptures about love, allowing them to guide you on self-discovery and spiritual growth. Practice mindfulness and reflection to deepen your connection with the essence of love within yourself and others.

3. What obstacles prevent you from embodying unconditional love in your daily life? Identify any barriers, such as anger, resentment, or fear, that may hinder your ability to express love fully. Be intentional in developing strategies to overcome these obstacles, such as practicing forgiveness, cultivating compassion, and setting boundaries to protect your emotional well-being.

4. How can you initiate a ripple effect of love that permeates every aspect of your world? Start by leading by example, demonstrating love in your thoughts, words, and actions. Look for opportunities to spread kindness, positivity, and empathy in your community and beyond, knowing that even the most minor acts of love can profoundly impact those around you.

5. Reread and list ways you can draw inspiration from 1 Corinthians 13 and other scriptures about love to guide your journey of personal and societal transformation. Consider incorporating spiritual practices such as prayer, meditation, and scripture study into your daily routine to deepen your connection with the divine source of love and wisdom.

As you contemplate these questions and strategies, may you be inspired to embrace love as a guiding principle and a powerful force for change in your life and the world around you. Remember, love has everything to do with it.

With gratitude and love,

Alisa L. Grace,
Founder of Sir-Rendered For Life, LLC

Live the Love You Have Learned: Love Letter To The Readers

Dear Flame of Love,

As you close the final page of "Love's Unconditional Revolution," I want to express my deepest gratitude for joining me on this journey of exploring the transformative power of love. It's been an honor to share these insights drawn from the timeless wisdom of 1 Corinthians 13.

Remember, the world constantly bombards us with distorted images of love—conditional, fleeting, and self-serving. But within these pages, we've rediscovered the true essence of love: patient, kind, selfless, and enduring. This is the love that has the power to heal, unite, and truly transform lives.

I encourage you to hold onto these truths as you step back into the world. Don't let the noise of conditional love drown out the quiet strength of unconditional love you've discovered.

Here's how you can continue this revolution of love:

- **Practice daily:** Consciously choose love in your interactions, even in the small moments. Be patient in the face of frustration, offer kindness to hurting people, and forgive freely.
- **Spread the message:** Share the principles you've learned with others. Encourage those around you to embrace unconditional love in their own lives.
- **Be a beacon of love:** Let your life be a testament to the transformative power of love. Shine brightly with compassion, understanding, and forgiveness in a dark world.

You might think, "Why should I read another book about love?" Because this isn't just another book. It's a call to action, an invitation to a different life. It's about unleashing a force so powerful that it can change not only your own life but the world around you.

Thank you for being part of this revolution. Go forth and love unconditionally!

With heartfelt gratitude,
Your Sister In Love

Meet The Author

Alisa Ladawn Grace is a retired school administrator, author, transformative life coach, and dedicated local missionary with an unwavering commitment to expressing, displaying, and demonstrating love to all. With over 30 years of missionary work, Alisa's life has been a testament to the power of unconditional love in a world marred by division, strife, and discord. She believes that love is the greatest force for change, and now more than ever, it is essential to offer a beacon of hope through love.

If you want to tap into the power of love and apply it to your life, read *Love's Unconditional Revolution! Unleash and Ignite the Transformative Power of Love*. This incredible book takes you on a journey to discover how the practical principles of love in 1 Corinthians 13 can be applied to every aspect of your life. From relationships to work, personal growth to spirituality, you will be amazed at how much your life can change once you apply these principles.

In addition to *Love's Unconditional Revolution*, Alisa has authored several children's books that emphasize civic engagement and personal development, including *Civic Heroes: Discovering Elections with the Supervisor of Elections*, *My Civic Adventure: Learning About Voting and Community!*, and *Unlocking Your Great Potential Within You: A Comprehensive Curriculum Guide to Nurturing Children's Meditation, Executive Functioning Skills, and Good Habits*. Through these works, Alisa continues to inspire and educate the next generation, shining a light of love in all she does.

- **Have you been conditioned to believe love is something you have to earn?**

  From toxic relationships to social media, we've all been exposed to influences that distort our understanding of love. We've been taught that love is conditional, based on external factors or meeting the needs of others.

  But what if there's a different way?

- **Discovering the revolutionary truth: Love is a powerful force that can transform your life and world.**

  In Love's Unconditional Revolution, you'll embark on a journey to uncover the practical principles of love in 1 Corinthians 13. Learn how to apply these timeless truths to every aspect of your life, from relationships and work to personal growth and spirituality.

- **Unlocking the power of true love and experience:**

  Deeper, more fulfilling relationships

  Greater peace and joy

  Breakthroughs in personal growth

  A renewed sense of purpose

  A life filled with abundance

- **Are you ready to unleashing the transformative power of love? Let the journey begin.**

www.ingramcontent.com/pod-product-compliance
Lightning Source LLC
Chambersburg PA
CBHW080913170426
43201CB00017B/2310